# Chronicle of
# a
# Corona Warrior

# Chronicle of a Corona Warrior

## (While at war with Corona in AIIMS)

**Ramesh Pokhriyal 'Nishank'**

*Translated by*

**Gopal Sharma**

*Published by*
**PRABHAT PRAKASHAN PVT. LTD.**
4/19 Asaf Ali Road,
New Delhi-110 002 (INDIA)
e-mail: prabhatbooks@gmail.com

ISBN 978-93-90923-87-8
**CHRONICLE OF A CORONA WARRIOR**
*by* Shri Ramesh Pokhriyal 'Nishank'



*Edition*
First, 2022

*Price*
₹ 300.00 (Rupees Three Hundred only)

*Printed at*
R-Tech Offset Printers, Delhi

# Foreword

## Roar of Life!

The man
Whose indomitable courage
touched the heights of the sky.
Whose belligerent passion descended
into the depths of the ocean.
Who climbed the Himalayas
and proved his mettle.
Who made the earth beautiful
With intelligence, prudence, effort!
It doesn't break apart.
It's stubborn like a steely rock.
It doesn't bow down before anyone!

These inspiring lines giving voice to the saga of mankind's struggle, determination, and accomplishing unique achievements by overcoming innumerable challenges are from the latest poetry collection of the country's eminent poet, story teller, politician Shri Ramesh Pokhriyal 'Nishank'. All the poems in this collection reflect the great pangs–*Mahavedna*– arising out of the immense calamity caused by Corona virus threatening the whole world. Just as *Sanjay* tells the eye-witness account of the battle of the *Mahabharata*, similarly this collection also re-tells the authentic account of the great battle in which, on the one hand, there is a very subtle but very terrible invisible enemy and on the other hand there is a crowd of humans and humanity! In this battle one side has utter destruction and on the other side there is the great passion of mankind.

The horrific circumstances arising out of the sudden attack on innocent human beings by the cruel Corona, the unfathomable ocean of pain, the young, the old suffocating for life...newly-wedded brides watching helplessly their honeymoon ruined. Mothers watching the innocent dying...in these poems, many heart-wrenching scenes are depicted in the poems so painstakingly written by the poet. These are capable of shaking and moving us to the core. The most unique thing about this collection of poems is that these poems have been written with tears more than the ink of the pen. As if they have spilled out and got moulded into letters and words within. The entire collection of poems appears as such a vast ocean of pain, in which many small islands of struggle, of courage, of compassion, of hope, of vitality, of humanity are also visible. Along with physical pain, Corona also brought the curse of remaining far away and dreadful loneliness from their loved ones. No one could even give a befitting funeral to his dearest one in the last journey. Many people could not even have the last glimpse of their loved ones. Many were compelled to mourn and remain away in other places and cities and were forced to grieve within themselves. All the helplessness, all the irony, all the pains are expressed in these poems.

To whom should I express my heart's agony?
In the turmoil of the struggle for life,
Life that is on the stake of death,
Putting shackles on someone's feet
Someone at home dying for his beloved.
Someone else gasping for breath...

Many poignant poems on the Corona warriors who are working day and night to save the lives of others in the terrible calamity also arouse faith in humanity.

In this horrific disaster,
In this terrible transition of inapproachability,
Our life is in the hands of those heroes
Those who risk their lives to save lives
Those who left their families
to save the families of others.
They add a historic chapter
to the book of human service.

This terrible epidemic has spared no one, rich or poor! Many poignant poems narrating the desperation, despair, immense pain, yearning of the poor reflect the human concerns of the poet. Even in the poems depicting the terrible pain, the poet never forgets to underline the courage, struggle, and valour of a man. The poet doesn't forget to infuse courage, enthusiasm, and hope in one poem after another. He tries to instill a new enthusiasm in man through many examples–examples of nature. Such poems fill any broken heart with new inspiration, new enthusiasm.

This dreary silence will break.
The spirit of man will triumph.
Man is very passionate;
He will stand up again
even after losing a lot.
The one who is saved
will finally move forward
with the same strength in the end.
Show of this mist of sorrow

will one day be over.
Man with pain in his heart
will smile again.

In this collection of poems, this terrible pandemic also gives a message to a man to create a new future by adopting a new lifestyle. There is also a lesson to be learned to protect nature and the environment, to avoid unnecessary exploitation of nature. In this way, this collection of poems appears to contain a wide world in terms of content in which a better man, a happy family, the essentials of relationships, the relevance of Indian values, a better country, and a resolution letter to make a better world also gets stored.

Although it is natural for everyone to be affected by Corona, yet a passionate, sensitive, alert creator has definitely affected a lot. Hundreds of small and big poems have been written on Corona, but the creation of a complete collection of poems is definitely a unique gift. These poems are not artificial poems; the poet himself has also been struggling with Corona and the complications after that. These poems have been written and composed during his fight back against Corona virus. Due to this also their effectiveness increases manifold.

This collection of poems is a valuable document proclaiming the resolve of victory of life in the fierce battle of life and death. The collection is a unique piece among the many works of Shri 'Nishank' which not only his fans will give their full love to, but all poetry-lovers will welcome it. It's my solemn hope and belief.

28 June, 2021

**—Laxmi Shankar Bajpai**

# Preface

## Emotionally Speaking!

I had never ever dreamt in my entire past life that such great calamity would befall on me and I shall be reaching out to my readers from the hospital bed. Of late, I have been at war with Corona. In the battle against this virus my physical-self has to withstand a lot of hardships and challenges and it's taking some time to regain health. I have been a fighter and have faced so many challenges before too but this is not an ordinary trial. The kind of struggle that goes on every moment of my life in my inner-self is very difficult to depict in words.

I am being examined every day and taken care of by a team of very experienced and able doctors. The entire day I endure great discomfort because of numerous tests and medical-examinations. The recurring thought of adverse side-effects of injections and medicines also bother me a lot throughout the day. On an average, I usually sleep just about three hours but now-a-days Corona has deprived me of even this little siesta. A strange kind of commotion goes on in my inner-self. Sometimes when I feel a little better, I steal some moments avoiding the searching eyes of doctors and nurses and look for news being circulated in social media scanning my mobile phone. The news of devastation is rampant all around because of the pandemic. Under these unfavourable circumstances, I decided to continue expressing myself through writing to give full vent to my strong feelings and to keep myself cheerful and optimistic.

How could I make doctors understand that relaxation is the only thing that disturbs me, though they have been advising me to take complete bed-rest? I understand them well as I am at war with the virus and also putting up with the side-effects of Corona.

How could I sit silent and watch helplessly the destruction all around caused by the pandemic? The eyes of millions of students were looking at me with great expectations. Millions of school-going children in their newly stitched uniforms were eager to attend their classes, but the uproar of Corona destroyed everything. Many innocent children lost their parents forever. Many parents couldn't see their children's faces and perform their last rites. A number of homes turned into wasteland. Still there is grief, sorrow and wailing all around. Nobody could even imagine that the life-force oxygen will be scarce to get and people will have to plead and implore for the sake of a mouthful of oxygen.

With the mantra of empathy and dialogue we have always transformed challenges into opportunities. I'm happy and also satisfied that the work of the ministry went on well from the hospital. During this testing time I was encouraged and my morale was always boosted by the inspiring and kind words of Respected President, Vice President and Prime Minister Shri Narendra Modiji, Speaker of Lok Sabha Shri Om Biralaji, Shri Raj Nath Singhji, Dr. Kasturiranjanji, Health Minister Dr. Harsh Vardhanji and several other senior members of parliament. This encouraged me and I got plenty of energy and power to continue my fight against Corona.

In addition I received hundreds of get-well-soon

cards and letters by social media, phones and other media. Their good-wishes encouraged me a lot.

My heart was flooded with thoughts and I was in a state of anger against Corona. Whenever I was in a position to write something, I used to scribble my feelings and emotions on loose sheets of paper. When I shared those little sheets of paper with my well-wishers, they advised me to get well first and write afterwards. They told me that I required complete bed-rest at that time. Their concern was genuine but I thought that I was going through this painful predicament at that moment and I should react and record it instantly. Now is the time when I am fighting for life–the uneven breathing, combating with the dreadful Corona–and the resultant hatred for the vile virus is making me boil with rage and fury. If I don't write it now and wait for some time, I will write a story. On the other hand, I know very well that writing has always inspired me to live and empowered me to withstand challenges. If I don't write during these testing times, I may go into unfathomable anguish due to frustration born out of pain. That's why I have tried to record in verse the moments of my struggle I have gone through there in AIIMS. It consists of all those events that I could hear and see and the events that moved me completely.

During those days, I had to endure many shocking news one after another. Shri Madan Mohan (ADG) and Balwantji of the ministry passed away. Shri Mohan Naithani, an adroit soldier of Sparsh Ganga Campaign, couldn't be saved from death though we tried our best. A number of great personalities associated with the fields of social service, literature, history, journalism, medicine and politics etc. were snatched away by the cruel hands of Corona. All of these had been my near and dear ones and I had a close and intimate relationship with them. Their untimely death left me shocked and sad.

Very often I was kept in the dark about all these sad happenings as I was also not in a condition to withstand the shock of the sad demise of so many people so dear to me.

Corona has devastated and destroyed the entire world. I developed a strange kind of hatred and rage against it. Day by day, this anger grew at a very rapid speed and it became very difficult for me to control it. On the one hand I was struggling to save my life surrounded with life-saving equipment and medicines in an ICU at AIIMS, Delhi and on the other, I was determined to defeat Corona in this duel combat.

During these tragic days young children lost their parents and elderly parents lost their dear young-ones. Just married couples were separated by the cruel blow of Corona. So many individuals were orphaned. Homes were turned into haunted-houses. Time was out of joint. Present lost its meaning and worth. Future was unknown and dark. Under such circumstances, it was natural for a sensitive and creative person to turn into blazing fire against Corona.

I have great satisfaction to see front-line corona-warriors working relentlessly. The valiant challenge wasn't an insignificant act. These warriors in their PPE safety kits were all around saving valuable lives. Their exemplary service to mankind will ever remain in our memory.

This is the reason that I dedicated the prize and honour given to me by a reputed organization Vatayan, London recognising my contribution to literature and remarkable social services to the Corona warriors of the world who have been working day and night for human welfare. I have great satisfaction in doing so.

I was extremely shattered and saddened when I got the news of Aditya Shastri and his young son's death. Aditya Shastri used to look after Bansathali Vidyapeeth (Rajasthan)–the largest educational institution for girls. It was a great blow for me to learn about the sad demise of the Chancellor of such a famed institution. When Aditya Shastri returned to India from abroad, his father Shri Diwakar Shastri told me at Bansathali, "I hand over my son Aditya to you, do take care of him." The news of Aditya's death was terribly shattering for me.

I had been getting the news of many prayer-meetings through Webinars conducted by a large number of my well-wishers for my well-being and speedy recovery. These messages not only conveyed pleasantries, but also provided me extra strength to fight the battle against Corona. I never imagined before that my fan-following and my readers spread in more than 60 countries of the world would express their concern and care in such an overwhelming way using different media. Their good-wishes and prayers and even their recitation of my songs and poems rejuvenated me greatly.

Sometimes I felt that there had been so many catastrophes before too but man had always conquered over those adversities. During adverse occasions one is tempted to write something worthwhile and inspiring for those who have been struggling to surmount great difficulties. I haven't tried to be extra careful about word-play, ornamentation and pedantry and have presented my agitated spirit and feelings in a very simple, inornate and direct manner. That's why these verses are expressions and overflow of my powerful feelings during my battle with the cruel Corona virus. I wish when you read these lines you also feel the intensity of rage and fire as I have been before so that all of us could wipe out completely this pandemic from our beautiful world.

I offer my sincere condolences and pay my tribute to all the souls that have left for their heavenly abode. I pray to almighty God that those who lost their near and dear ones, those who are affected by its heinous attack and are still struggling and all of us should get abundant strength to get rid of this evil. We must win this battle soon.

I am convalescing and regaining my physical health and strength. I am feeling cheerful and healthy now. I put forward this book for your reading from the edifice of All India Institute of Medical Sciences (AIIMS).

**—Ramesh Pokhriyal 'Nishank'**
AIIMS, Delhi

23 June, 2021

# Contents

# The Himalayas can liberate us from this Pandemic

Can the Himalayas liberate us
from this grave predicament?
The *Vedas, Puranas*, and *Upanishadas*
Environment–Nature–*prakriti*
In addition, and a step ahead
*Ayurveda*, the greatest life-science
Will all these not make the world
free from this great evil?

Can't this grand movement
very affectionately called '*Sparsh Ganga*'
Not stand for the safety and security of mankind?
Only for this day this movement was born.
I hope and wish for its imminent success.
The world looks at it with hopeful eyes.

Experiencing severely the challenge of Corona crisis,
I am admitted in AIIMS, Delhi.
And believing firmly in my mission
The resolution of '*sparsh Ganga*' will be complete.

—AIIMS, Delhi
4 May, 2021
☐

## Your Arrival is of no avail

O shameless Corona!
Why do you arrive again and again?
It's of no avail, I say.
I don't know why?
And then, return helplessly tired;
Sheepishly subdued.

How many times have you examined
my resolve and patience?
How many times have I attended
your multifarious challenge?

When you return every time
disheartened and sullen;
Why do you turn up
again and again unannounced then?

Now get lost. Go!
Help the helpless.
Fill in them with courage and righteousness.
Can't you live with peace and happiness by doing this?
Can't you let the happiness and pleasure
flow in the entire universe?

You are free to wander and meander.
Go and travel aimlessly in
My entire body

Go in, inside my veins–
My breathing—inhale and exhale
Enter my person...
Every chamber of my body
Let you be in there.
My heart and soul will entertain you too,
Rejuvenate you too,
And fill in you a new universe.

Just you forget giving pain to others
and be my guest as and when you desire.
I stand here with open arms.
Take it from me, I tell you the truth.
My doors are open for you forever.
Just forget giving pain to others.

—AIIMS, Delhi
Room No. 705, 2 AM
5 May, 2021

☐

## Address to Corona

Where've I accepted defeat?
Where've I defended the scare?
Ever been following bravely
My life-passage struggles calmly.

I question your arrival to me
Your return shamefacedly is also ensured.
Dare to ask me my resolute resolve...?
Unaware you yourself,
How do you enter this way?
But, I overpowered you too.
I will decimate darkness
By turning myself into steady flames
to sow the seeds of hope.

Never have I slept in slumber
How could I now?

Look!
In this utter darkness
I've ignited the lamp of life.
Look!
At your unsolicited pitiable arrival
I've conquered even you!

—AIIMS, Delhi, 7 AM
6 May, 2021

□

# Not an Ordinary Battle

It wasn't an ordinary battle
Never knew such a great difficulty
Struggling every moment for life
Never inferred before indeed.

But once again I proved to myself
Defined once again the life-force I got.

I continue fighting my battle
All alone single-handedly with courage.
Day in and day out, day and night
Challenging and defeating
the invisible enemy of mine.

In every falling breath
I am filled with a new breeze.
I become my own power
to overpower my pain.

Many a time when devastating dilemma
Weakened my tender heart
I collected myself and
Gave solace to it too.

Corona!
Victorious I feel
Defeating you boldly
After unbreakable fighting back—*Tapasya*
For eleven hard days
I return back home as a Corona Warrior...

—AIIMS, Delhi
6 May, 2021

□

# Pandemonium

When there is chaos in every direction
When the cries and shrieks are rampant
When the sobbing and wailing pierce the heart
And the helpless beings lose all hope.

Come; let us beam an earthen lamp
Place a glowing lamp out in great tempest
Does it seem impossible?
But let us give it a try.

One who is broken and down,
Running inanely from pillar to post
Come; let us hold his hand firmly
That is abandoned, declaring him insane.

It's difficult time, testing time
Shrieking and sobbing increasing
The thread of life tied with
the gaping of the gasping breath.

Give this lean thread a gift of togetherness;
the gift of closeness to breathe
Give the renewed trust to those hands
That are in need of your helping hand

The balm of closeness in general
Removes pangs and pain indeed

All the despair is taken away
Within an instant.

Come, let us spread together
The message of humanity.
Come, let us behave lovingly
By sharing our pain and pleasure.

—Himalaya Bhavan, Delhi
12 May, 2021

□

# Ode to the Cloud

Listen to me, O Cloud!
Your thunder and lightning;
Your rumble and rousing
Unannounced and unseasonal pelting rain
Dear Earth is frightened of you.
All your roar and howl
Shrieks and screams, scare
Mother Earth.

Though your arrival brings happiness,
Yet the way you come now
In the garb of dread and threat;
We're all scared of you.
The entire landscape is dotted with fear
Because of your daring look.
Your deadly thunders
Turn the heart of the Earth
Into a melting strainer.

Listen to me, O Cloud!
The Mother Earth is passing through
A difficult time now.
In pain she sobs day and night
Taking note of her universe's grime

O Cloud!
Are you too in a pensive mood?

Are you too crammed with pain unbound
considering the Earth and her people in pain?
Are you too losing confidence
sensing the time so hard to bear?

Pay Attention, Dear Cloud!
Just wait for a while.
Advise tenderly to the hazy mist and obscure fog.
Instruct them all
to spread in different directions
in the open infinite sky
like the snow-white flakes
And paint a beautiful picture
On the blue canvas.

Listen, the venerable one!
Do not torture the helpless men any more
They are struggling hard for a fresh breath of life.

I invoke you, Dear Cloud!
Spare and save
The men struggling for life
Don't torture them anymore.
Spare India's gentle-folk
My country's innocent people
From the death-knell of deadly Corona.

—Himalaya Bhavan
13 May, 2021

☐

# A Pleading to the Mother Nature

Mother Nature! Listen!
Look, your sons are groaning and moaning,
Getting new lease of life in diminishing respirations
Mother, let the milk of your motherly love trickle
pacify them, eliminate their unbearable misery

Grant gulps of Oxygen sky-high
Provide patience earth-like
Provide morale tall as the Himalayas
Transform the heart like a pious lake.

Supply tenderness from flowers
Multi-colours from rainbow
Invite heavenly gods if you wish
To turn difficulty into opportunities.

Mother Nature!
Fill up the deep wounds
Of the sieving heart
At least, grant them
A little boon for their good Karma.

Decimate from the earth this hurt and pain.
Establish the element of Truth.
O Mother Nature!, we plead
Return us those happy, smiling days again.

—Himalaya Bhavan, Delhi

13 May, 2021

□

# On Getting Help

Engaged in the battle for life,
Struggling to catch some breathe,
Engulfed by deadly Corona,
Lying on a bed at the seventh floor of AIIMS
I was there...tired, weak and feeble
But not broken and defeated.

For a while in a pensive mood
Just to look outside
I reached up to the balcony.
For many days couldn't see the open sky,
So I gazed at the beaming clouds keenly.

Outside in the void there was strange noise,
Devil Corona's assault was seen on every side.
I found darkness of despair around
In the din of this difficult time.

My wandering gaze stuttered at a sorry sight.
A woman drifting here and there helplessly,
impatient and eager to get help from anyone
with folded palms, imploring towards onlookers.

Perhaps someone of her own
was in dire difficulty and needed help.
She went from pillar to post very feebly
So many times her morale and spirits weakened.

I was myself engulfed in the mire of Corona,
twisting and turning in dejection not able to help others.

O God! Please provide some help to her
It was my appeal to the merciful God.
Repeating my prayer sobbing endlessly
Her hopes shouldn't get shattered, O God!
Her dear ones should survive
The sobbing, weeping little ones
shouldn't be left in the lurch forever.

Then, all of a sudden,
An elderly man walked towards her.
He signalled her with his hands
and pacified her greatly.
She wiped her tears with the sides of her *sari*
and went away fast in the opposite direction.

Thank God, I'm ever grateful to you.
You have illuminated the lamps of support
by protecting and safeguarding her broken hopes.

Her panting heart got
the blessings and support
It seemed to me, my Lord!
As if the lotus of your grace
had bloomed in full swing.

—AIIMS, Delhi
14 May, 2021
□

# Unconquerable Man

In the roaring silence around
People shrieking and shouting
Beating the chests for their dear ones
Struggling for even feeble breathing.
People making a lot of hue and cry
For not able to see the faces of dear ones
at their last moments of life.

Cruel Corona!
Oh! You have created such ruckus
tortured and killed mercilessly
so many throbbing happy lives.

O Cheat!
The present day may be yours for a while
By your deadly destruction,
the entire world is moaning.

But listen to me, O the greatest evil!
We are human beings.
Our great indomitable spirit
touches the heights of the sky.
Our aggressive commitment
goes deeper in the depth of the sea.
We climb the lofty peak of the Himalayas
to let the world realise our indomitable spirit.

By dint of our skill and intellect and hard work
We turn this earth into a beautiful place.

Man can't be shattered into pieces
Neither can he weep inconsolably.
He is stubborn like an unbending rock
Never bends before any mortal like this.

Yes, his tender feelings
make him sentimental at times;
His caring heart is also filled with
the flood of tears uncontrolled.

Yet, he never gets defeated
by hitches and snags around
Never runs away fearing
Storms and tempests abound.

Be sure! He will stand again firmly
keeping his personal grief aside.
He will march forward in life
keeping the sweet fading memory
of his dear departed in mind.
Sure to say, he will always try to realise
his unrealised dreams.

A resolute man he is
Reconstructing the destructed path again
He will sing the songs of creation once more.
Will win over desperation forever.

—Himalaya Bhavan, Delhi

15 May, 2021

□

# Daybreak that takes away Darkness

In the clasp of this deadly disease,
the dark night crouches.
The heart and mind filled with frightening dreams
searches a friend ceaselessly.

Let the night be dark and long,
As much as can be
Let many lives wander and
fade away their priceless lives.

But,
The bright-rays emerging from
The determined sun
Will pierce the heart of the dark-night
And the golden aura will bring
An era of joy.

Birds will chirp in
Their nests
In the loving lap of Mother Nature
The earth will shine.
When the sun rays will touch the heart.

In the dark of night
The struggling mind will be reassured

By the ray of hope.
The power of man's effort in the struggle for life
Will defeat this pandemic.

This war of life and death comes
In many forms and shapes.
Man takes up every challenge.
When and where did he get scared of them?

As ever before, this time too;
He will win this battle by his
resolute courage and patience,
He will be called The Universal Man.

—Himalaya Bhavan, Delhi
16 May, 2021
□

# No Room for Grief

There is hardly a man on this earth
that hasn't faced difficulties.
Very often, these adversities break the man,
shatter him and move him greatly
in the grief of someone so dear to him.

Under these circumstances,
There are people, who are so grief-stricken,
broken and helpless;
They turn their lives towards utter doom.
They endlessly wait for the dear one,
one that will never come back again.

But,
I've seen some really heroic people.
They never allow grief to overpower them.
Let the loss and grief be immense and devastating
But, they never succumb and give up their lives.

It doesn't mean
They never grieve for those dear ones
who lost their lives at the Corona's altar.
They weep and cry inconsolably for them
The dead ones, memories linger
and fill their eyes with tears.
They collect those memories
in the inner chambers of their hearts

and devote their time in the service of people
suffering from this deadly virus.
They turn the sad memories into their strength
and leave no place for grief.

These brave-hearts fill the vacuum
with their creative impulses
So that their tender heart could never sink
Into the unfathomable mire of grief.

New creations everyday can erase
emptiness and void
in the dull and lifeless existence.
When the colours of creation
are splashed around,
one gets the purpose of life-divine.

—Himalaya Bhavan, Delhi,
18 May, 2021

□

# Call to Nature

Listen to me, Mother Nature!
Ignoring you,
no one can possibly live.
For you;
It's not impossible to take this anguish away.

Do not place the bed of thorns
In the path of your dear ones.
Don't pierce your thorn of neglect
in the wounded heart and body.

Agreed, you have embellished
this world around
But, where is your subsistence
without human beings?

Take away the anguish
by your natural force.
Destroy this dread and misery
from the bottom of our hearts.

Let the new buds of life,
germinate in our hearts.
Let the love-nests around,
be filled with the twittering abound.

Decorate this pallid world
Brighten it with colours galore
Decimate this disease for ever
With the *sanjivani* existing in your womb!

—Himalaya Bhavan, Delhi
19 May, 2021

□

# Grieving Heart

Today the heart is somewhat grieving,
to some extent disinclined and unwilling.
Even amidst the dance of soothing rain,
in the enveloping fog around
searching eyes look keenly for
someone lost and gone.

The pulsating heart vibrates
as a peacock dancing.
The little bird hums in the tree
a soulful song.

Someone sings
a melodious song to express
his heart's pangs.
With a faint smile I too hide
My bitter-sweet pain
touched by it.

Oh! The music of the birds
on the bows of love
A loving squirrel hops around
playing hide and seek.

The damp leaves of the trees
take me forcefully
to my village.

There is an uncanny numbness pain
in my entire body.
All of a sudden I contemplate,
lost in the lilting songs of nature.
I wish to sing along with the parrot
moving backwards and forwards
and mingle along with Nature forever.

Let it be for a while at least
But in the company of nature
I will forget the deadly sting
of the Corona virus.

—Himalaya Bhavan, Delhi
20 May, 2021

□

# Conflict

Man's conflict with unwanted enemy
goes on for centuries.
It changes face and takes different garbs.
Today again we plan to conquer it.

Perhaps it doesn't realise well
Man is made of five elements;
and with the power of his devotion
can transform and bring life even in stones.

This Corona has challenged
such great indomitable warriors
Those that can pierce the rocks
Men of steel and great resilience.

Today again the battle is between darkness and light.
Erasing the blemishes painted black by Corona,
The ray of light will be the winner again.
Flaming blaze of fire will burn into ashes
this evil Corona disease forever.

—Himalaya Bhavan, Delhi
21 May, 2021

□

## Grant those Days Back

Those innocent prattle and chatter,
and the innocuous laughter;
That used to sneak out in the street stealthily
To carry on friendships
are engulfed and enveloped
in the desolate, noiseless corridors
speechless and isolated.

That cycle-race and the strolling around,
the hide and seek in the playground,
the naughty activities,
everything has come to a halt.
The sweet home is turned into
the school, and the playgrounds;
Even the lanes and streets around
inhabit the tiny little home now.

Today this tiny abode
Safeguards children
Childhood chatter resounds here
The entire day.

Looking at the infinite sky through the balcony,
the childlike heart soars higher.
Even implores to bring
the moon from the sky.

This heart is eager in rain
And wants to play in mud and mire
With friends, to imagine and dream
the moon and the sun.

—Himalaya Bhavan, Delhi

22 May, 2021

□

# This Time too Shall Pass

You have seen difficult times,
This time will also pass.
I encourage myself repeatedly,
This moment too shall pass.

There was a time when I had a brawl with time.
There was a shackle of thorns all around me.
But I never stopped my march, never lost confidence
and climbed the hill of life till its peak.
Smiled even amongst thorns pricking hard
knowing well that this time shall also pass.

Was surrounded by storm, engulfed in swamp,
yet never lost faith ever in life-divine.
Got intrigues many in return of love,
Yet you never let me fall from grace.
Always managed a smile in adversity;
Knew fully well that this time too shall pass.

—Himalaya Bhavan, Delhi
22 May, 2021

□

## Enough is Enough

This frightening battle for breathing
Beyond imagination,
perhaps no one ever thought before
For breaking, impeding gulp of air
Commotion everywhere
Birth and Death are the Truth of life
But, what kind of death is this?
No near and dear around you at all.

People struggling and begging door to door,
Faces, pleading, appealing, requesting
Stooping on their knees
Babbling incoherently, flattering helplessly
To save lives is so precious indeed.
Even after staking everything
They got nothing but emptiness.

Brutal Corona extinguished
the brightness of their lives
Flowers blooming in full youth withered
Corona! You have shattered lives.
When the deep hennaed hands had to take away
All her ornaments and the marks of wedded life.

Oh! What a tragedy!
Just now these newly born innocent eyes
have seen her infinite sky.

Just now children have had a love-cradle prank
in the lap of the darling father.
All of a sudden the love-knot broke.
The rope withered,
and the childlike cheerfulness
shattered in an instant.

O God!
Enough is enough,
Let the black episode of this catastrophe
Be over now.
Listen to these moaning prayers, God!
Do not allow this mayhem to continue any more.

—Himalaya Bhavan, Delhi

23 May, 2021

□

# When the Future Comes to Know

All are motionless and stunned,
but my heart is disturbed
The quiet wind wails insolently,
By the terrible cry.

With whom should I reveal?
Who will tell me this?
In the commotion for the life-force—Oxygen
To whom should I tell my heart's tale?
Someone is on the vortex of life and death.
The other is imprisoned and chained in his abode.
Someone for his dear one is
in pain to get her respite from
the deadly virus and
trying to give her a new lease of life.

All are shattered by Corona wreck,
All have got hurt.
Directly and indirectly,
Each and every one is wounded.

When someone will tell this hoary tale
and others will listen to it.
They will surely find it unbelievable and
label it a horror story
born of the figment of imagination.

—Himalaya Bhavan, Delhi

24 May, 2021

□

# Vegetable Vender

In the poignant silence all around
With heartening news
The mind is getting very disturbed
Seeing the people losing the battle
The mind is losing its patience.

The daily newspapers are filled with
Desperate words from beginning to end.
Not a single line that gives solace and comfort
is found by the meandering tearful eyes.

One day,
In the fog of flowing tears
I saw a vegetable-cart.
A vocal vegetable-seller
placed a bag in front of a door,
And this routine went on for a few days.

One day, opening the door
a woman came out.
"Don't place vegetables like this, vegetable-seller *Bhai*,
My husband is laid up with Corona.
Not a penny has he earned this month
I have no money to pay you.
Therefore, don't place the vegetables anymore."

The vegetable-vender smiled and replied—
"I know, sister, what happened to you people.
Only a very lucky person will be one
who has not been touched by the pandemic.
I can understand your helplessness and pain
Hungry children crying for food
must be making you very sad.
You have been buying vegetables
from me for a long time
This has remained
a source of my earning and livelihood.
You prefer to buy vegetables from me than
large shopping complexes nearby
I remember every day, sister!
When my throat gets hoarse with shrieking
in scorching sun and hot climate
You always gave me water to drink
Realising the toil I undergo
to make both ends meet."

"When you are under distress today,
how could I turn my eyes away?"

"That's why I keep vegetables for the day
Even though I find the doors closed."

The woman folded her hands in reverence
With eyes filled with tears
She spoke no words, she couldn't.
Isn't this incident an example of humanity?
Can't it break the dome of negativity around?

—Himalaya Bhavan, Delhi

24 May, 2020

□

# The Fog will Disappear

When the deep fog obstructs
the rays of the Sun and his entourage;
and the rays too stay put for a while
allowing the fog to continue its pranks.

The dark fog then gets confused
as if it has stopped the shining Sun
As if it has dissolved the brightness
of the glittering glimmers in itself.

But, within a flash
The Sun comes down from the confused sky
to the land of reality.
The sharp arrows of the Sun
Scatter the mist and the sunshine spreads
far and wide again.

Similar to what this Corona imagines.
It doesn't realise the might of a more powerful weapon.
The man's indomitable will,
that will decimate it forever.

By the attack of unconquerable determination
The end of Corona is imminent.
In the great war in the transitional time
Man's victory is on the cards and sure.

—Himalaya Bhavan, Delhi
25 May, 2021

□

# The School that waits

Many days, months and years have passed
To tell the truth, your gleeful laughter
I miss a lot and feel deeply sorry
Gazing fervently the empty lanes
I'm still standing there anxious to catch
A glimpse of you
I'm your own lovely School.

Runs continuously in my heart
The joyful beats of your feet,
The memory of those invisible footprints
Even today my heart beats.

I am still alive
Living on your fond reminiscences
In the hope
that one day
The destruction of Corona will stop
And the innocuous childhood hidden at home
Will march towards me.

I remember vividly
How in the embrace of my cosy lap
Your childhood used to bloom
You always hid yourself in my bosom
Leaving your mother's lap.

When your tender fingers
drew casual lines,
And your teacher gave a helping hand
To complete your drawing,
That victorious muslin smile I loved the most
Your small gain made the entire class clap.

From the alphabet learning to life-philosophy
You had gone step-by-step
climbing the school's stairways
Went ahead and renewed
research with innovation all.

Those classes,
Where you used to learn brick-by-brick
The life-lesson for good
And used to have a good time with friends
Your naughty and frank pranks.

That veranda,
Where unblemished hearts
Bloomed in love and affection
The promises and vows of friends
used to be the witness of abiding love.

The sure success sutras for life
Were first uttered around my green precincts
Defined the bond of teacher-student relation
In accordance with our priceless culture and tradition.

The cosy green grass court
Where the sweat of your hard toil
Water its greenery.

Life-less it has become without you
That *Velvet Bugyali* ground.

Evil Corona's ruthlessness
Tied tiny feet and kept them at home
The life of countless lads remain
Uncertain and wasteful for the time being.

I'm confident
Slowly but surely
This wide-spread ill-omen
Will die and lapse.
In front of Corona Warriors
Corona-cruelty will expire too.

And the school-bell
along with the temple-bells
will ring and ring again
The school-gates that have been waiting for long
will reopen once again as before.

—Himalaya Bhavan, Delhi
26 May, 2021
□

## Break Your Silence!

O *Tripurari Shiva!*
It's enough, break the silence now
Stop watching the world with half-shut eyes
Look, your world is in turmoil
Venomous flames of Corona
Taking over the world.

O Kind *Neelkanth Mahadeva!*
Consume the venom once more
Place this poisonous disease
In your all-encompassing throat
And save this existing world
Take away all pains of all the creatures
Save this earth that is dying in pain.

*O Triyambak!*
No more, no more
We can't witness this tragedy
Any more.
The wounds of Corona
are no longer bearable.

We beseech you our Lord!
Spare some time.
Leave your meditative trance.
Break the silence.
Leave looking at the world with half-shut eyes.

—AIIMS, Delhi
26 May, 2021

❑

# O Aditya! You've been Entrusted

Dear Aditya!
Say, it was all a lie
The news of your departure
Was someone's delusion
How can I believe it?
How can someone godly like you
leave the world so abruptly?
How could the life of one
who was a life-saver
leave so fast?

Oh! Such pity!
Is it true indeed?
Your father's words turned into
An unfulfilled vow?

My Aditya!
I still feel the touch of your hands
The palms in my grasp
I hear the words of your father
Still drumming in my heart.

You will leave so suddenly this way
Will the eventful era end so abruptly?
Never had I dreamt all this

I recollect and remember those days now
Your numerous dreams
tied with each and every single *Bansathali's* brick.

I remember everything
And search for you
In the fog
With the eyes hazy with the tears flowing incessantly.

—Himalya Bhavan, Delhi
26 May, 2021
□

## An Angel

Amidst this chaos and pandemic
Surrounded by this deadly virus
Our lives are in the hands of brave-hearts
They stake their lives to save ours.

They have left their families and homes
To save other's home and hearth
In the book of service to humanity
added one more resplendent chapter.

In the hospitals in their white uniforms
Busy day and night they are the godly figure indeed
Others in the *khaki* Uniforms stand in
Sun and grime
Rain and shine,
True angels saving lives.

They are on an endless journey.
On their way there is risk at every step.
Never bother about future,
They challenge death directly
They are saving lives risking their own.

I salute such brave warriors
I greet them again and again
They have laid their lives too for humanity.
I bow my head several times
for these godly-angels.

—Himalaya Bhawan, Delhi
27 May, 2021

□

## One Day will be that Day

One day something like this will happen.
When even the mere particle of yours
will not exist.

Your destructive plans will be turned to dust.
Your name will not be there in the world.

You have tested the limitless patience of man.
Manly personality tempered with.

You brought up a duel with
Such a creature that has often defeated
Even the Grave Holocaust.

The ruthless barbarity,
the devastation caused...
You probably don't know well
What a disaster you have created!
What did you achieve by all this?
Brutally torturing us and
extinguishing the lamps of millions of our homes.

But know full well
that your catastrophic intentions
will no longer succeed.
Rock-steel man will never be weak
And will stand before you ever.

What have you got?
So many children orphaned.
So many wives widowed.
Millions lost their ones
because of your brutal deeds.
But you must know for certain
Your vicious designs will not materialise
Men of steel and rocks
Will not weaken before you.

—Himalaya Bhavan, Delhi

31 May, 2021

□

# Light such a Lamp

Come, we shall decorate our Earth
In Unison we shall renew it well.
And then we shall establish a new world
In the lap of our Mother Earth.

The snow-peaked Himalaya will shine
By the blazing rays of the Sun
The lazy hill will melt
Under the holy feet of Lord Shiva.

When the dark clouds
Splash their moving eyes,
the magical fountains
will steal the heart in abundance.

The ripe harvest hurling its golden attire
will offer the crop a plenty.
The bees will hum profusely
after touching the flower-buds.

By the sound of the fragrant wind
Koel will sing her melody.
Good luck songs will reverberate around.

In this land of ours
We shall spread humanity once again.

And light such a lamp that
Fills our hearts with gaiety.

Cruel Corona will also lose
The world will celebrate victory,
will hoist the flag of life,
Man will sing songs of creation.

—Himalaya Bhavan, Delhi,
31 May, 2021

☐

## Man will Smile as before

The time is out of joint now.
All around there is silence of the graveyard
But once the time passes
One day this too will go away.

The temples of learning
Will reverberate with laughter and fun
Childhood will bloom again
In the now deserted lanes.

Deserted roads
Will come alive again.
Holding hand together
Will tell the tales of their
Happiness and sorrow.

This silence of the graveyard
Will break into pieces
The man's courage will win.
He is a very brave and passionate,
will rise again from all this.

He will take the life forward
With the renewed zeal
With whatever he could collect in
Losing so much in bargain.

The haze of sorrow, you see!
One day it will be gone,
Burying deep all his grief
Man will smile as before.

—AIIMS, Delhi

2 June, 2021

□

# One Day it will Stop

Commotion, lamentation
Crying and weeping
This upheaval due to helplessness
Death of the near and dear
Rage and resentment coupled with tears
Shivering of those pleading hands
Fighting and quarrelling for a puff of air
One day it will certainly be stopped.

It will stop, no doubt
And will leave a lesson
A deep contemplation, along with
A thought worth reflection.

People will start living again.
They will consider their home and family
As the only treasure they have.
Instead of running aimlessly
From pillar to post
They will try to live peacefully
With their families and friends.

Will start again
Nature worship
Dense afforestation,
Then waving trees
Will be able to exhale fresh air to breathe.

O God! Please stop it here now
all this great calamity and turmoil,
this black episode-pandemic
Man is ready to live again
even after losing so much.
Got the value elixir of life.

—AIIMS, Delhi
2 June, 2021

□

# Neither Now, nor Then

When were the circumstances favourable?
To test me they always remain hostile
Either they know me or my persistence
Or they desire to train me to make me strong.

Let it be, whatever may be in both the cases
My heart has become stronger than before
Noticing my great power of tolerating pain
Even time favoured me all the while.

This time is life's hardest one
Great hardships I bore before
Neither did I stumble then
Nor I will slip now
These bouts of adversities too
Got my love abundantly.
I never got broken down
Neither now, nor then.

—AIIMS, Delhi
3 June, 2021
□

# Momentary Illusion

When the horizon is enveloped by dark clouds
Filled with water,
They may be under the illusion that,
they have obstructed the Sun.
They roar like drunk
Making frightening faces
Wander fast in the limitless sky.

But their illusion remains for some time
The illusion to block the mighty rays
is transitory and brief
When the sun shines
on thunderstorms
Falls on dark clouds
Then the clouds
will rain heavily.

Dark clouds filled with water
Slowly turn into white stripes
Fall down and fly away
The arrogant cloud
meander and appear
To challenge the Sun
By enveloping the sky
But scatter around and disintegrate.

Due to the raze of the Sun
The same will happen to
this great monster.
It will also burn into ashes,
when millions of lives will curse it.

—AIIMS, Delhi
3 June, 2021
□

# Will Defeat all Difficulties

You have taught me
To fight with all kinds of difficulties,
Taught me to step forward
Always making way in difficulties.

Never imagined that you will
ask me to face these troubles.
Never approached these machines—
The factory made Oxygen.

But you have seasoned me and
turned me into steel.
I promise to you in earnest
I shall cross this peril too.
My life! To tell you the truth,
I've loved you with great passion.

—AIIMS, Delhi
4 June, 2021
□

# The Power of a Lamp

To remain eternal
I've seen Nature's struggle
When the season arrives
It decorates itself.
When the calamity advances
It gets wounded.

These catastrophes:
Avalanches and landslides
Rivers overflowing
Forest-fire blazing in rage
Roar of the Earth in the form of
Worrisome earthquakes.

Ruthless uprooting of trees
This beautiful land of mine
Very often goes undetectable
Sometimes by floods, other times by famine.

So much this Nature tolerates
Not now, but for years together
Continues enduring calamities
Notwithstanding all these deadly commotions
Nature never ever has lost her self
Even in complex conditions
She sows the seeds of creation.

Even the splitting mountains
Could never vacillate its inner trust
No flood could put off
The ever sparkling lamp of
Hopes and wishes.

He trusts that
From the forces of destruction
The power of the lamp of hope
In my heart is many times more
by whose will the whole creation moves.
He is the protector of my life.

—AIIMS, Delhi,
4 June, 2021

□

# I Trust my Inner Self

In the lap of Nature
On the high branches of trees
When the bird makes its abode
Knowing full well
That under the open sky
Its nest may be flown away by wind
Cruel rain may dampen it
Enemies flying all around
may snatch away her happiness
But the little bird is not afraid of challenges
and makes its nest there.

Leaving its kids under the protection of
Mother Nature
It goes in search of grain
Every moment under the shadow of risk
When does that bird forsake patience?

She has complete trust in
Its unblemished heart
That makes her victorious
In the endless battle for life
This inner self can make it possible
In the company of Nature
The birds lurking, fly high.

—AIIMS, Delhi
5 June, 2021
□

# The Gift that the Earth gave

If you desire to get something
in return of your charity and goodwill
Just meditate on
That earth by whose incomparable donation
Our existence is made possible
Ask nothing in return.

Have you ever thought about it?
The earth that looks after us all the time
Has no personal desire
The manure of philanthropy is deep rooted
In every bit of the earth.

The earth that gave us grain for sustenance
Trees to breathe fresh air
And shelter to live
In her lap every colour of life
Every shape of life
Blossom and sparkle.

Though she bears the burden of countless creatures
On her breast and suffers silently
She gives out gold, when her heart is pierced.

Contemplate, what have we given her in return?
Though we take so much throughout
The gift of life given by mother Earth is the greatest gift
Has anyone else been comparable to it?

—AIIMS, Delhi

5 June, 2021

☐

# Corona-Pandemic will be Defeated

Whenever God decided
To test your endurance,
He placed on your difficult pathway
Thorns added with pebbles.

Cloud of sudden crisis
Dominate your existence,
So your soul is disappointed
Not deviate from the path
Blaming God and cursing fate
is not the right approach.

Getting disheartened and dismayed
during such difficult time
is called cowardice.
This is the time that turns brave-hearts
into indomitable warriors.

Trust in our own-self can
Let one win the world.
Perhaps this pandemic
Doesn't know well about
our resistance-power and fighting spirit.
Doesn't recognise
our trust and belief in God.

I'm so conditioned with
struggles and challenges,
that these difficulties seem to me
pretty small.
In front of every new difficulty,
My renewed consciousness
Awakens again.

Look, if not today then tomorrow
This Corona too will surely be beaten by me;
Will accept the supremacy of my iron-will
And the victory-garland
will be placed around my neck.

—AIIMS, Delhi.
6 June, 2021
□

## Tolerance-Limit

It has happened in life many times before
When time tried to break me
Tried to scatter me too into parts
Like a scattered glass.

But I
When did I break by the punch of time?
I was not scattered then, nor am I today.
Even though the maze of conflicts
Got me entangled for a while
But I've never wavered in life.
I have always reached the limits of resistance
And came out of every maze.

From momentary wounds,
There is bound to be infinite pain
But my pulsating heart
Never loses patience in pain.

The culmination of patience and suffering
Takes me out of trouble.
Always gives me divine power
To deal with hard times.

—AIIMS, Delhi
6 June, 2021
□

# If it's to be Scattered

Sometimes I think
Scattering also has its own style;
If man falls apart or
falls into depression;
he can't handle himself
and his creative-*dharma* comes to an end.

But I perceive
Whenever this Nature disintegrates,
it spreads out in different forms.
It brings out something new every time
And embellishes itself in many more ways.

In the morning, it brings out a new day
By spreading the sunrays
The fragrance of flowers is dispersed
And every part of the body is
activated and excited
The earthy smell keeps us
Connected to our land.

If the seeds of creation
Are dispersed and scattered
Life on earth will make
the expectation of new sprouts to grow.

The flame of the lamp and its glow
will shatter the illusion of darkness.

The Nature makes the night beautiful and bright
By scattering stars along with the moon
Spreading the rays of the moon
It makes the moon-lit night cool and fresh
Splitting the deep darkness of it.

If one desires to scatter
Scatter and spread like the Nature
The Nature spreads her immeasurable love
Makes the land fertile
And brings out new creativity in the world.

— AIIMS, Delhi

6 June, 2021

□

# Will Come out Soon

Hear it! Cruel Corona,
That's the power of my clenched fist
My shield in this battle every moment
We both know that
How am I in every passing moment?

The conflict of different ideas in me
Runs day and night
This heart that trusts God
Complaining about him
Several times.

Whenever the heart is weakened for a while
The past flashes before the inward eyes.

For oft, I've risked my life
Holding life at stake.
Setting my intentions ahead in mind
I've worked even in adverse times.

That's why life has ever given me
Her boundless blessings
I'll come out of these days too
My conscience has given me
Confidence every time.

—AIIMS, Delhi
7 June, 2021
□

# Illusion of a Dark Night

When the dark night wears a sheet of conceit
Slowly embraces the evening
And in the frenzy of darkness
Covers the earth.

It envisages that on the ground
It has established its empire.
The entire universe has been imprisoned by
The fear of obscurity to the living world.

But it's illusion is shattered
After some time
By that illuminating moon
That rises from the edge of the hill.

The cool breeze in this flood light
Looks very beautiful
And the black night hiding the face
Wander around and everywhere.

And lo and behold!
Just after some time passed
The golden rays of the Sun arrives
From the East riding
A chariot drawn by horses seven.

Listening the knock of the day-dawn
Where did the night go?
Where's its shadow?
In an instant, its designs had faded
To shatter the delusion of the dark dusty night
The Sun-God had arisen with all his glory.

—AIIMS, Delhi

7 June, 2021

☐

# Climb, Fall, Climb again

Sometimes when desired success eludes
Even after working so hard
Success can't be yours,
When you sit sullen and tired.

Take a look around
See little ants
Relentless hard work
Twice its size
Carry a load
Climb up and down
Fall and climb again
To start
Until then
In its goal
Don't reach and succeed.

Do you know?
How does an ant climb so high?
Even after falling so many times
It takes courage to climb once again.

Because it has never seen helplessness
What will the people say?
This question doesn't terrify it.
It has made up its mind
Climbing is the set goal of its life

Even after falling a hundred times
Its heart never wavers.

It never leaves patience
Concentrates each time
On the path to success
Even in failure
Never disheartened
And in the end, finally
Gets success paramount
It never leaves its life
On the destiny unknown
Never dragged life doing nothing in forlorn.

—AIIMS, Delhi
8 June, 2021

☐

# Be an Antidote

O King of the Mountains with a bright gray aura!
Look towards us
Today once again this world
is suffering from the venom of Corona-pandemic.
This pandemic is swallowing up
The agonising world.

O the Mountain-king—Giriraj!
You've always swallowed
The poisonous winds;
In your exhaled breath
Life has been given back to us.
Your melting gives satisfaction to the world.
The entire world gets relief.
From thirst and dryness
Your beauty energises
Our body and heart.

O Great Mountain!
Protector of creation!
So dear to Lord Mahadeva!
Be once again the shelter of all
Be antidoto for this venom
By placing it somewhere else
Where it should have been.
As blue-throated Neelkatha!

O My dear Himalaya!
Become a life-saver
By enduring the gloomy earth.

—AIIMS, Delhi
8 June, 2021

□

## A Solemn Resolve

The duel that broke out with Corona
Stands as an impediment
in the way of my campaign
Ignorant of my extremes
This cruel falsehood stands
adamant before me in conceit.

Though I never broke in pain like this
Tolerated even intolerable pain
without a groan
The pain tried to squeeze me every time
But I kept taking care of myself.

Today too
When I am being surrounded by
So many machines and equipments.
The machines surprised me by breathlessness
Upset everyone, alarmed all others.
I collect myself giving auto-suggestions
And control the uncontrollable shooting pain
Travelling from top to toe.

Hiding the times to overcome this crisis
I have resolved.
With trembling hands, I hold my pen
And keep this time alive too
by writing these lines.

—AIIMS, Delhi
9 June, 2021

□

# A Lament Born Out of Pain

So greatly I've to hate Corona
That the hatred born out of
The entire world included
Can decimate it
Uproot it in entirety
Its heinous and heartless atrocity
For ever and all!

—AIIMS, Delhi,
9 June, 2021
□

# Because I'm a Mountain

Struggling to defeat this deadly virus
I'm here in this huge building of AIIMS
It has been overcoming me
And I was trying to defeat its every attack
It kept me down
And every time I went down
Stood up again after each fall.

My conscience has been fighting it.
'I'm a mountain' has been saying
Every moment of it.

I'm that mountain
One who is self-respecting
This is the story of carefully collected feelings.

I've seen many holocausts
Have often suffered burns
and withstood tremors
Got habituated of tremors and tribulations
Withstanding tremors and tempests
is in my habit now.
So many times blazing flames have played
Hide and seek with me in vain.

Yes like a phoenix, even in the ashes
I'm resettled

Even after the catastrophic storms
I'm calm.
Even on shaky ground
I stand firm.
Taking in the poisonous air
I've also become a *Neelkanth* sometimes.

Do you know why?
Because I'm a mountain
Terrify those who make the harsh noise
I roar like a lion.
I'm a mountain.

—AIIMS, Delhi
9 June, 2021
□

# Have to Get Back

In the whole earth, this soot of Corona
Has darkened so many happy homes
So many innocent children are left orphaned.
So many mothers lost their apple of the eyes.

With its destructive intentions
It tried to shatter me too,
How dreadful, frightful and horrible it is!
It tried to overpower me again and again.

Its every assault reminded me
My past struggle and resistance.
The power I got from all past strikes
Gave me strength to overpower it again.
I never stumbled, even on steep climb
Never faltered or gasped, even for a while.

Today all these memories hold my breathe
Provide me ample speed
When little physical weakness ensues,
It gives me patience.

Even though this virus was hell-bent
to break me momentarily
Yet I also persisted to wipe out the soot.

I have to settle my account of its tyranny
What is lost in these days
Gotta get those back.

—AIIMS, Delhi
10 June, 2021

□

# Destruction of Corona Monster

When the entire body was in pain
When from the pain was hurting greatly
When my patience was tested by God
In me too there was turmoil
Created by this worldwide pandemic
My patience was also frightened.

Like a wounded warrior on the battle-field
I too was not disheartened at all
Never lost patience even for a while
during the uneven rising-falling breathe.
Endurance was never lost;
My conscience defeated its heinous objective
The effect of its venomous arrows went to waste.

Corona!
You are a stigma on this fertile land.
Determination only will destroy it,
With mountain-like strong intentions only
This monster will be destroyed.

—AIIMS, Delhi
10 June, 2021

□

# Emerge in me

Whenever this creation has been overburdened
And has come under the threat of devilish demons
Whenever the corrupted mind wreaked havoc here.
*O Shiva*! You have broken your meditative trance
Of so many centuries.

Ever become *Gangadhar* to the earth
You saved the earth from being
Fragmented by the mighty velocity of the Ganges;
Because of the immense flow of the Holy Ganga
Ever become a *Neelkanth*, you saved so many lives
By consuming venom.
Ever became *Ranchandi* to the effect of primal-power
Within himself and stroked the chest.
*O Mahadev!*
Today is the time of your ultimate dance—*Tandav*
The moment of destruction of the brute has arrived.
*O Ashutosh!*
Burn into ashes the conceit of this demon.
*O Trinetrdhari!*
Decimate the evil heart of this fiend
Erase the very existence of the life of this evil one.

*O Avinashi!* Annihilate its body-aching
Life threatening mortal sparks;

Blow it with the gusto by the clout of your command
All those difficulties caused by it.

*O Shiv Sambhu!* Come down in my body
In my heart that remembers you
At the time of such life-threatening pain
O Lord! Make a way into me.
Hold on,
Blood in veins, in arteries
I call you every moment.
*O Chandramouli!* Grant me that cool feeling
This pain really hurts.

Enough is enough, Lord!
Awake now! Save this world
Let the crying men go back
Into the world of fun and frolic
Chirping with happiness
Into that love-filled world.

—AIIMS, Delhi
11 June, 2021
□

# You inspire me

*O Himalaya!*
I've kept my heart as pure and unblemished
As your white spotless clothing.
Amidst dark shadow of a million adversities
I've kept myself awake and alert.

Whenever I feel lonely in my life
You always keep encouraging me
You too have been facing challenges
Always single-handedly fighting alone.

Inside me like you
Lies an abode of tender concentrated feelings
Hey *Himaraj*, Listen to me,
These are the powers
That have embellished this life of mine.

*O Himalaya!* Your steadfastness
Has ever been my inspiration.
The culture and civilisation
Flourishing in your foothold
Has always been venerable for me.

My dear Himalaya!
I have an unbreakable bond with you
Your bewitching beauty mesmerises me every time.

—AIIMS, Delhi

11 June, 2021

□

## Always Collected Myself

There was a sword-like edge on the ground
under my feet;
But when time stirred me
I walked carefully.
Burning coals were spread on the ground
But I suppressed the pain by clenching my teeth.
I swallowed my tears in my eyes
never to let the world see them at all.

Perhaps risks too like me so much
Difficulties threaten me now and then
I have been always patient
This saved myself
And defeated death so often.

Even though the enemy disguised many times
Many had a clash with me
Others spewed poison
In the invisible periphery of my heart.

I have always escaped my enemies unhurt.
The bout of time also put stumbling blocks
But even after little faltering,
I've been balancing myself again.

—AIIMS, Delhi

12 June, 2021

☐

# The Earth didn't Lose Patience

This is a very painful time
for our dear earth.
This pandemic is lethal
as it mutates again and again.

From the outbreak of the pandemic
this land was injured
The scarcity of vital life force—Oxygen
There was helplessness all around.

Trying to somehow control
this patchy condition
But all of a sudden it rose again
like terrible tempest
We were safe inside our homes till now
But now it was like the roof had gone.

The tempest was destroying the grounds
The cloud-burst at the mountain cracking.
As if the world was going to an end
The mountain itself was going down.

Man is under so many pressures and challenges
Perhaps God is also testing our steadfast patience.

This earth has faced
so many challenges

So many times before too
There have been many tales
Buried deep in her heart.

This earth never let her patience go
Even when everything was gone.
Man can neither weep throughout
Nor should he.
Earth and man in disturbing times
have always sown again
What is called
The seeds of creation sublime.

—AIIMS, Delhi
12 June, 2021

□

# Oh, What a Pleasure!

I am in AIIMS
Trying to regain my health
Whenever I find rest and time from
continuous medical check ups,
I start reading the poems of the book—
'The Touch of Nature
in the vicinity of the Himalayas'.

Ignoring the cacophony of medical equipments
I reach closer to the Mother Nature
Where the all-pervading calm gives great relief
To my restless mind.

The cool breeze of the fountains
Enlivens and refreshes the heart and soul
In the soothing rain of *Saawan* month.
My soul also get stirred to watch
A tiny squirrel hopping and jumping
In the relaxing rain.
The bird picks up the grain of rice
Scattered in the courtyard and takes
Them to the nest.
She comes back again
and dances in the rain for long
I am so fond of her strolling and rolling
Her twitter and mutter surprises me greatly.
Her twittering chirp creates curiosity.

Everything so well-arranged and well-presented
Nature has given to us
The right way to live well
Only those who are lively and blithe
Live fully well with Nature.

Oh! What a pleasure!
So much is filled with the elixir of life
I am engrossed in these
Forgetting the troubles of battling illness
I'm lost in these.

—AIIMS, Delhi
13 June, 2021
□

## Fetch the Stars

Come, let's dream once again
And see with half shut-eyes
Decorate this Earth
Like a beautiful bride.

Decorate the trees
with tender buds
Garland it around
By the flowing Ganga.

Spread a bright flower-shawl
Over her encompassing head
Embellish the entire Earth with
The green attire so grand.

Take shining moonlight
And relaxing rays from the sun
Pluck bright glowing stars too
And then beautify her forehead.

Let the twittering birds
Sing the songs of welcome and goodness
And share the message of this Earth to all.

Message of verve of life
Of the strongest determination,
The message is to fight bravely,
Of unfathomable devotion of the mind;
Then you will see, the Earth will sing again!
Humanity will flourish once more!!

—AIIMS, Delhi

13 June, 2021

□

# Human Conflict Continues

Whenever on earth
demonic and wicked ways
begin to lay a web of thorns
Sadness, pain and despair begin to spread
Then Lord *Mahadeva* takes up his *Trishul* in hand
Lord Rama takes up his bow and arrow
And resonate the cosmos by their rage
*Arjuna* also takes up his *Gandiva* Bow
And aims towards killing the demons around
By the power of *Nav Durga*.
And aims towards killing the demons around.

Even the might of the pen has also been used
To strike defensively against the tyranny
Ever engaged stylus has always remained
A great weapon against the corrupted mind.

Even today man's struggle with the pandemic
Continues and goes on
We are on the way towards victory
Over *Dharma* by *Dharma's* ways
For the victory of the Universal Man.

—AIIMS, Delhi
14 June, 2021
□

# Indomitable Self-respect

I'm battling death
Even though I am struggling for life,
Yet living with Nature
Forgetting the pain prick of sharp needles
In recollection of the memory of the Himalayas.

I was born in the lap of mountains
So the intentions will also be of steel
Not a sand-house made on a sand-dune
That is scattered by the mere blows of the wind.

In my upbringing, in place of the velvet bed
I got rough ground of struggles
And the sky wide-open
My bleeding feet made me dwindle
But my indomitable self-respect remains as ever.

The unmatched beauty of the Himalayas
Lure me so often
In its heavenly glimpse
My heart takes life's lessons.

One who takes refuge in its abode
Gets knowledge ultimate
And turns into a Universal Man
By following the path of
Spirituality, faith and culture.

—AIIMS, Delhi
14 June, 2021

□

## What do you know?

You have been playful and happy
Have been beautifying the life with happiness.
Left no stone unturned and worked day and night
For the sake of a golden future.

Cruel Corona!
You couldn't tolerate this contented joyful life
The world of these innocent ones got shattered
By your deadly attacks
Within a fraction of seconds
Children lost the protection of their father
The shining vermilion on the forehead of a bride
Was washed away by her tears
At the sudden death of her husband
Because of your act unkind
You have smeared gloom on every dazzling face.

Oh! Don't you get disheartened by
the groans of these innocent ones?
The people beating their chests
Cries of others calling their dear ones
Don't you get upset by all this?
Doesn't it pierce your heart?

O Evil Demon!
You are simply heartless.
How do you know what a family is?
For children their father
is their beautiful world.

—AIIMS, Delhi
15 June, 2021
□

# Destiny too Turned away

The commotion rampant around
During these heat waves and inclement weather
The mind goes completely blank
hearing shrieking and groaning voices.

Cruel Corona!
So many homes got shattered
Because of your destructive assault
So many protective strong hands
Are lost forever.

Ill-fated mother dreams of
her son's marriage procession.
Her dreams are shattered,
when she is awakened.

The solitary lamp of her home
has gone off by your poisonous turmoil
Oh! The ailing mother cries in vain
as if even destiny has turned her down.

By your ruthless brutality
You have massacred many innocent lives
You have made millions of lives cry for their dead.

These millions who are wailing and weeping
Their fire of fiery tears will destroy you too
The curses of the groaning heart
will also decimate you forever.

—AIIMS, Delhi

15 June, 2021

□

## Can't Scare

In this challenging time of life
The conflict of ideas is creating turmoil,
Gathering courage to crush
Corona's corrupt mind.

Now-a-days the unsolicited pieces of advice
Are continually showered on us.
How to tell that from the inner rage
My heart is so heavy!

This fire of anger will consume
The sly corona.
And every bit will take account
Of the tragedy.

I'm calm, but I'm angry inside.
Want to destroy
The stronghold of Corona.

The flood of my pain will
Taken away its hellish plans.
My turmoil will wash away
Its catastrophic intentions.

The pain, the continual seething ache
can't frighten my resolute ways.
Stubborn I am really too much beyond thinking
That's why, no attack and hit given by you
will wither my majestic spirit and patience.

—AIIMS, Delhi

17 June, 2021

□

# Uproot it Now

Outside of my room, heavy lightning
And thunder of clouds
Torrent of rain like a flurry of arrows
As if there was a tornado in the sky
terrifies a lot.

*O Meghraj!* Have a lot of rain!
Let it rain so much
That the existence of this Corona
Get destroyed by it completely
With the rumblings of the earth
Go shatter it.

Stop its destructive speed
Merciless to terrorist impulse
Crush its poisonous hood
O Cloud! Save the life on earth.

The fierce heat of its toxic flames
Extinguish it by your catastrophic form.

Finish it.
The entire clan of this man-eating Corona
Erase it.
Uproot this devil from the root.

—AIIMS, Delhi

17 June, 2021

□

# Why have you Devastated Everything Like this?

*Sawan's* knock is at the door.
How many desires did both of them have?
Will swing together in this rainy season
These beautiful dreams were seen by both of them.

Deeply drawn mehandi—the henna colourant
Sparkling red vermilion,
Arrived in red ceremonial pair of clothes
Everyone congratulated the couple to be safe
And wished them a long life.

It was only a few hours
Enjoying the joys of the new world
Death knocked the door
In the costume of Corona
Dragging away all the happiness.

The sinful Corona destroyed
The newly-wedded couple.
Wreaked havoc with blazing fire
Like a blazing fire it took away all
Oh! It was the darkness personified.

When at home the groom felt suffocating
And his breathing was uneven and choked
Oxygen level dropped

Relatives ran here and there
Looked out for a hospital
Neither the hospital nor Oxygen they found
The rampant pandemic was at its peak
Its death knell was everywhere being heard.

What an ill-fated time!
Just wedded bride
With all her paraphernalia
Makeup and looks
Got wrapped in darkness and decay
Within eight days of her wedding
Her husband was snatched away
By the iron hands of nasty Corona!

The sinful corona shattered her dreams
His family and the world
It was just awful to see
Her tears overflowing
Taking along all her desires
O Tyrant!
Why have you done this to her?

Her curse will be for you always
Each time she groans in private or in public
You are cursed and will not remain in peace
Your days are numbered, you take it from me.

—AIIMS, Delhi

17 June, 2021

□

## Orphaned

Corona, Because of your forced entry
Everything has come at a standstill
Whoever was wherever
has stood there shocked.

Couldn't move any more
Just near the doorway
Sat on the floor and slept
Childhood slept on the floor unattended.

The curse of that helpless labourer is on you
He hid his face in shame
As he couldn't get work because of you
And his children couldn't get a morsel of food
He cried in shame and powerlessness
When the family slept without food.

O Sinner! You've been snatching lives
From all around
Taken away breathe from some
From some employment
Taken away life in haste
And given them eternal sleep instead.

How will these labourers experience
They have no work
No food at home to eat

Great commotion for everything
Nothing left for sustenance.

He waited everyday for
The news of lifting the lockdown
In the hope of getting a handful of coins
And just survived.

But you cruel Corona
You didn't agree to this
He was the only bread-earner at his home
What was his fault?

O Cheat!
That labourer got upset because of your misdeeds
How could he continue watching helplessly?
All his family and children hungry and disturbed
He couldn't withstand their pain
He was defeated before your evil deeds
And took his life by himself.

You are not only a murderer of this labourer
You are the murderer of those happy children
They are orphaned by your cruel deeds
Their curse will chase you wherever you go
Will bring your doom very soon.

—AIIMS, Delhi

18 June, 2021

□

# What will be the Answer?

An innocent bubbling daughter
Just four years of age
Unaware of Corona and its tribe
Was shouting repeatedly for her mother
The black shadow of Corona was destroying
Her playful life and world of dreams.

Her doctor-parents were busy
day and night in the care of corona-patients
Corona! Both of them got infected
By your venomous sting.

They consoled each other
Remained in the hospital
Keeping their daughter at home
In safe custody
But I missed her a lot too.

When they were exhausted of your venomous attacks
And couldn't sustain more
They left for their heavenly abode.

Shame on you, Corona!
You have been giving us these wounds.
What do you get by leaving
innocent children in lurch.

The doctor couple left the world
Holding each other's hands
The life-savers couldn't save their lives
As they were attacked by your heinous spears.

Their orphaned daughter's care was
their paramount concern,
when they breathed their last.
What will be your reply to this girl
crying inconsolably for her mother and father?

—AIIMS, Delhi
18 June, 2021

☐

# Two Month Young Flower Withered

O God!
Haven't your heart trembled
Looking at this pathetic sight?
Couldn't you guess the cruelty of
This rascal called Corona?

Prayers and pleadings for so many years
Their home got a child's jingle
Each one in the family
was elated at the birth of a child.

Corona, by your dreadful attack
This two month flower withered
The mother's milk waited in vain
for the lips of the newly born one.

Your ruthlessness didn't stop here.
You snatched away the right to cry and wail
Clasping the baby to the mother's breast.
In hospitals her body rotted,
Nobody touched her
Cruel Corona, why did you make all so heartless?

The open sky grieved and cried bitterly that day
When the semi-decomposed body

was put to rest by others.
Even the earth wavered and felt horrible,
When her heart was dug open
and that innocent bud was put to rest.

The trembling hands placed near her dead body
A bottle filled with fresh cow milk
To compensate mother's warmth
A blanket was wrapped around too.

Every fist offering a handful of dust
was filled with curses for Corona
Mother was all fire and rage
cursed you time and again.

Corona! You have a cursed life
Would be disgusted even to himself;
Millions of lives will be hurt
Your downfall is ensured.

—AIIMS, Delhi

18 June, 2021

☐

# Let me say Something

If the seething pain from within
appears during these difficult days;
Let that pain overflow in every vein
If the time wants to pass with fast speed
Let it pass fast and uninterrupted.

The rising anguish has spilled in the eyes.
If it falls, let it fall.
Anger also fills in agitated mind,
Let it be scattered in the form of words.

Do not stop my expressive heart
The rising tide of the heart
If my feelings wish to express in words
Let them do so to ease the mind.

—AIIMS, Delhi
18 June, 2021
□

# The Soul Trembles

There is the silence of the graveyard
in this three-storey mansion.
Every brick of the building is a witness of
The gory game played here.

Father used to be so proud of his four sons
The family used to be full of merry-making
Grandchildren and others lived with fun and festivity

They loved each other
Lived under the protection of the parents
Well to do and rich
Ready to sacrifice for each other
Tied together with the cord of cordiality.

That May, the pandemic spread like wildfire
The elders at home under the grip of deadly virus
Dragged by the dragon disease they all died.

Oh! Cruel Corona
Why did you inflict such an atrocious act?
Those suffering in your fire;
Why didn't they get help from each other?

For two days their dead bodies were burnt
The very existence of the family was being consumed
Children were speechless, they lost words

To express their anguish and pain
Nobody understood what was happening.

Hey! The slayer of these children's happiness
How many corpses will your bloody roar swallow?
Seeing such a scary scene
Everyone's soul trembles.
This massacre of yours, the earth covered with ashes
Lives buried, people sighing and sobbing
This cruel game of yours will result into
Your disastrous death too.
You will get the curse of so many humans
Wailing and weeping and shouting for help
In the fire of their burning woe, Corona
You too will also be consumed with dust.

—AIIMS, Delhi
18 June, 2021

□

# The Punishment of Misdeeds

Extremes have limits too.
Even calamities face insurmountable difficulties
In the thick of pain.
When the scorching fire of the sun
Exceeds the limits of extremes
And the entire world burns
The showers of *Sawan*
Brings coolness to the smouldering fire.
When this *Sawan-Bhadon* rain rumbles and pours
Reach the limit of extreme
Floods of water makes the mountains full
Cloud bursts everywhere
Willing to take everything away
The deluge of these overflowing rivers scares,
A restless man's heart trembles with fear.

This orgy of a few days suddenly then it calms down too.
Warm sunny days then fall apart
This earth shines again.

Like this, you have also reached to the limit
Now the chapter of your atrocities will end;
You won't win over this man of steel.
Holding the basket of curses, hatred and disgust
You will be punished for your misdeeds.

—AIIMS, Delhi

19 June, 2021

□

# Dead-Bodies Yearning for Loved Ones

Waiting outside that mortuary
Not living humans rather
there were piles of corpses
No place in the crematoriums now.
How much time will it take
to start on the final journey?
Man on his eternal journey went with great fanfare,
Got all the rituals done by the hands of near ones.

Oh irreligious fellow, Damned wicked Corona!
Your savagery threatened everyone
Every ritual and rites, *Dharma-karma*
All faded away.
What can I say about living beings?
Even the dead are made to cry.

They died in pain inflicted by your severe attacks
No sooner did they breathed their last
They were wrapped in a plastic sheet
The relatives that waited for their safe homecoming
Just waited now for their loved ones' corpses.

Its heart wrenching
Unbearable and shocking
Corona, your hellish deeds

Make the volcano of anger erupt.
This wrath full of hatred for you
Will consume you
Even after death these tormented corpses
Will take account of your wickedness.

—AIIMS Delhi

19 June, 2021

□

# Be your own Guide

Try to find out the secret of life
Where good is defeated by evil
Find out such a wonderful battlefield
Where this great battle takes place.

You are the image of your own thoughts
You are the melody of your own voice
Be your life's own mouthpiece
Search for your journey's ultimate goal.

The noise of the crowd often tests
The patience of the thumping heart
Wander deep inside your conscience
Find out the reason for it.

The spotless and pure heart
Gets hurt by the arrows of deception and pride
Hunt for an ultimate weapon that could
Destroy all these adversities and hardships.

—AIIMS, Delhi
19 June, 2021

□

# A Requiem: Whom will we wait for at our Doorsteps?

He was the only heir
To his old parents at home
Just twenty seven years of age
So young and full of life
Nurtured and pampered
By struggles and difficulties.

He was the apple of their eyes
He was the shine in the lives
Cruel Corona!
Don't you know?
He was their last hope.

Their lives remain blank and subdued.
It's over for years to come
Who will they live for?
The will to live is also dead.

Heard with blood in the eyes
The cry of that mother
who received the news of his death
first with disbelief ignoring it.

Just show his face for once
And I will wake up my son

By my tender loving kisses four.
He usually sleeps for a long time
I'll kiss his forehead and wake him up.

The helpless father banged his head
And grieved inconsolably.
Who will listen to his admonition?
To whom will he stand and wait at the door now?

Shame on you Corona!
I spit on you with disrespect
You have got the whips of thorns;
You bleed and rot
Let the fire of curses fall upon you.

You must get the bite of every groan
Emanating from mother's empty womb
O Sinner! You must get a worse death sentence
In the abyss of disgust.

—AIIMS, Delhi
20 June, 2021

□

# You will receive my Curse

Vile, evil and wicked Corona!
In your first toxic wave
Father left the family forever
O sinful!, you were not satisfied with this
So you suffocated the mother too.

Both daughters stricken by your meanness
Took mother to the hospital by a rickshaw.
Sensing the crumbling breathing of mother
They both kept pleading for help.

O cruel one! Your naked orgy
was laying corpses all around
In the chaos for getting life-force—Oxygen
Nobody was listening to anybody.

Both of them were with the mother at this moment
The next moment they would fall at someone's feet;
at the corner of the hospital
Looking for a place for her.
They could neither get a hospital bed
Neither the innocent got any help
Crying in the scorching sun
Took mother back to their home.

Your cruelty killed mother
begging for a gust of air

She died on the way home
The last resort to daughters.

Now the mother had got her final sleep
Daughters' world was ruined forever.
From your raging ambushes
Their world was completely shattered.

Their eyes were filled not with tears
But were blood-red because of frenzy
Their hearts were angry broken and wrecked
All because of your terrifying misdeeds.

These burning dead bodies on the funeral-pyre
Their blazing everlasting flames
will become a volcano of destruction
for your doom.

In the time of great vengeance
In this great deluge of massacre
You too will be destroyed
You will get curses in abundance from
The people in pain and distress.

—AIIMS, Delhi
20 June, 2021
□

# What a Terrible Calamity!

Death is imminent, eternal
But so gruesome?
So painful
that even death itself is terrified.

Lightning and thunder,
The sky was dusty.
Parents will return sure,
Yet the heart was uneasy.
But it was waiting to pounce.

Sinful Corona was ready to attack
He became a victim of Corona's atrocities.
That was a scary dark night
He was all alone at home
And had to call for an ambulance for himself.

Wretched Corona!
The horrific thunderbolt of the helpless sky
Collapsed all of a sudden.
The earth sighed and exclaimed thunderously.

Doesn't your heart shudder
in dread to look at the barren homes?
Don't you tremble to see deserted homes?

You swallowed the son waiting for the parents.
Seeing this, the creator too was shocked.

It wasn't last journey of one single person
Had piled up, stuffed up bodies around.
Everyone was defeated by Corona.
When the dead bodies were placed on the ground
Dead corpses of his unfortunate parents clasped with
The lifeless body of the son.
All three of them were clinging to each other
Until their turn.
They were together in the death-knot
Till they were separated to be one with the dust.

Oh, what a great calamity!
Ah, what a great disturbance!
O evil one!
How terrible is the outbreak caused by you!

O Sinner one!
Your heinous sin will burn you with curses
Worst monster! You will receive an apocalyptic curse
From these tormented souls.

—AIIMS, Delhi
20 June, 2021
□

# Valiant tale of Humanity

Created from the pure thoughts and chaste conscience
Be such systemic syntax pure and simple
Don't be wrong in the flow of words
Become such a pure grammar.

Always give the pledge of security
Be such a strong cover
Let the decorated head of steadfastness
Be such a beautiful adornment.

Purify the path of truth
Become such a rare equation.
Couldn't forget even the giants
Be such a unique memoir.

Eradicate hatred from the heart
Be such a loving integration
In the valiant tale of humanity
Be a supernatural divine incarnation.

—AIIMS, Delhi
20 June, 2021
□

## Tormented Bangles

In the suffocation of toxic winds
In the clutches of unbearable pain
She was living in hope every day.
Waiting in the vortex of Corona
She was sipping the draught of poison.

Corona! In your death-knot
Her husband was tied
In your terrible catastrophe
He stood between life and death.

There were so many tasks to be completed
He alone could perform.
He alone could take them
On the flights of their reasonable dreams.

Corona, you are
a sinner, disgusting and cursed one.
Your cruelty has strangled him.
He groaned and ultimately died.

Every brick of his ruined home
Will drown you in the ocean of hatred
The widow's broken bangles will pierce in you
And will give you agonising death.

—AIIMS, Delhi
21 June, 2021

# Holding the Bundle of Life on Head

He was enduring every moment
The intolerable pain given by Coronavirus
In the hope of getting cured
Counting his days on the hospital-bed.

Worried about his family
Thousands of miles away from him
Nobody of his own was there around
That made him cry again and again.

After some days
When he got well and reached his room
With the smile of victory on his pale face
He was shocked to know
That he lost his job meanwhile
The Company was closed
Someone phoned him and gave this message.

What would he do now?
How will his life go on?
How will he inform his family?
So many questions with no answer he got.

Whatever he earned and could save a little
All that gone in treatment long
Nothing was left to sustain and live
The family was there too to feed.

There was no one to help him in the city
There was no way but returning back to his village
He marched towards home due to no choice left
Not a penny in pocket, hardly anything to carry
He started the long journey just on foot.

A small bundle on his head
And the scorching sun under his feet
He went on and on
Hating his wretched life.

He went on and on unmindful of the difficulties
When tired, he took shelter under the shade of a tree
Wept bitterly very often at the loss of everything
The pandemic was nothing but great pandemic for him.

Helplessness was written on his face
His head had a bundle of belongings
And was also filled with
the shuddering thoughts of dark future ahead.

He went on walking for a month or so
Reached home somehow
With his broken dreams and tired body
Positioned himself on the ground
And never got up again.

The family around in a state of shock
Wailing miserably to look at his motionless body
Devil Corona's shadow was writ large on
his otherwise motionless face.

—AIIMS, Delhi
22 June, 2021

□

# Bier Instead of Palanquin

April 25th was the date agreed
And the preparation for wedding just started then
All of a sudden everything was stopped
The turmoil of Corona destroyed everything
So painstakingly planned.

International flights were cancelled
The groom will not be able to reach
The girl was shocked to hear this
Mother's wish will now remain unfulfilled
She should have given her daughter in marriage
Before she breathed her last.

Everyone was in tears looking at
The helpless mother on death-bed
But this sly Corona didn't bother.
It was determined to destroy everything.
It had already decided to destroy it.

Amidst the strict rule of Corona
Now marriage was impossible at the moment
Many dreams were broken
Last wish left unfulfilled
All the preparations were in shambles
The moments that the mother had kept aside
Even those were over.

The day set for daughter's wedding and farewell
That day the mother left for her heavenly abode.
Abandoned the world forever.

What would have happened to that family
That was not bidding sister farewell
But was forced to pick up mother's bier.

Oh! What a heart breaking scene!
Even the sky above was shedding tears.
Sinner Corona! This injustice was because of you.
All this is the result of your atrocities.
The world is crying because of you.

—AIIMS, Delhi
22 June, 2021
□

# What a Devastating Tragedy!

I was watching his movements for a long time
Listening to his worried words carefully
I couldn't resist and asked him.
"Brother is in ICU."
His worried voice divulged
His concern for his brother.

"No other is there in the world for me except him
He is the only support of my life.
He was in mother's womb when our father died
Mother also departed the day he was born."

"I was myself a very immature child then
Unaware of the miseries of being an orphan
Mother's funeral pyre extinguished
But the fire of the belly could never be composed
It has been killing us slowly but surely."

"Almost all the relatives turned hostile
Left both of us unattended and orphaned
So many times I thought
that I should sink along with my brother
Or burn myself into ashes
and get rid of these predicaments.
But looking at the innocent face of my brother
I couldn't muster the courage to do so."

"He is the only heir of my parents left
Thinking all this I saved myself from this crime."

"I have been a single-parent to my brother,
His ultimate guardian and care-taker all,
I have left no stone unturned in the care of my brother,
He is the only source of my joy and life.
My brother is more valuable to me than my own life,
I have dedicated my entire life for his upkeep.
This sinful Corona has wounded him now
And I am crest-fallen sharing his pain
But looking at pain and grief everywhere
I will go back to my duty."

"Sir, you are yourself in pain
I'm sorry to bother you.
Noticing your sympathetic attitude
I couldn't stop myself
and told you my sorrowful tale."

"Sir! I will take all pains
And knock every door
for my brother's well-being.
As I'll never be able to live without him."

Oh! My God!
What a tragedy, what an irony!
I am myself trying to come out of this mire
Struggling to come out of the dense forest of pain
How could I console him properly?

Yet I collected my courage and called him aside
I consoled him lovingly:

"Your devotion, dedication and commitment
will not go waste
Go and serve your brother with patience
Everything will be alright in due course of time."

He kept mum and moved his head in affirmation
Hiding his tears somehow;
I shared his grief and pain
and prayed to God for his brother's speedy recovery.

—AIIMS, Delhi

23 June, 2021

□

# I've Come Defeating Death!

Never imagined and dreamt
Such calamity will befall on me.
Under the strict vigil of machines all around,
my body will remain so helpless.

Corona, I have been enduring
ill-effects of your attack;
Every moment of my life,
withstanding extreme excruciating pain
radiating from head to toe onwards.

I've measured thousands of kilometres
walking bare-foot
I never got tired
Neither collected breath ever
gasping on the climb.

Today I am laid up motionless on ICU bed
Pierced by so many synergies and tubes
Can't move even
Have I become so helpless?

Medical checks every five minutes
The sleep of the eyes has run away somewhere..
Haven't slept during days for long
In nights too my siesta remains elsewhere.

During such hellish moments
The recollections of past linger on
A storm of thoughts in the mind hang around
I've defeated death many times before too
This memory of my fighting-spirit boosts my spirits.

Though the agonising pain gives me severe concern
From momentary restlessness and falling breaths
The mind is suddenly shuddering with fright
Up and down breathing pattern terrifies me.

But I have firm belief
I shall overcome and subdue
all these grief-stricken days
I will certainly defeat all deceits and trickery.

—AIIMS, Delhi

24 June, 2021

☐

## Salutation to Corona Warriors

In this horrific situation of Corona
The kind of conflict my conscience face
makes me upset a little.
Even the very name Corona irritates me.

In this ward of AIIMS
I'm fighting this evil enemy
Those who are engaged day and night
in this battle are also being
Watched by me intently.

I am examining those warriors around me
Their gentleness, patience and pursuit
Is worth noticing and noting.
Never let them waver even for a while
Engaged in the service of mankind
These Godsend angels evoke respect
In the hearts and minds of all.

How difficult it must have been
To know the plight of their own
They too are attacked by dreadful virus
But these warriors serve all and gain their reverence.

I too get confidence
Seeing their devotion to duty
Looking at the pinnacle of their dedication
My heart is filled with reverence for them.

These Corona Warriors are worthy of salute
For their passion for the service of humanity.
I too salute them all again and again
For what they did and have been doing.

—AIIMS, Delhi

24 June, 2021

□

# My Stylus went on

My Stylus! My Pen!
O Destiny!
How much patience the Creator has given you!
In the storms rising in the mind,
In the whirlwind of thoughts,
In the sea of depression,
In the cry of rising pain,
In the edge of the sword and my naked feet,
In the groan of broken dreams,
In separation from the beloved,
In an impenetrable array of deceit,
In the poisonous fascination of crooked laughter,
In the presence of pretentious love,
In poetry born out of heartache,
In stalemate, in retaliation for betrayal,
In moments of momentary joys,
In the granules of a cheerful mind.

This stylus of mine,
Sometimes drowning in the ink of tears
Sometimes burning in the fire of pain
Sometimes scorching in the ever vengeful flame
So sometimes the crooked laughter got tricked
But this pen went on day and night
Without lodging any complaint or grumble
It goes on and on, on the loose sheet of papers.

—AIIMS, Delhi

26 June, 2021

□

## So many Feelings are Veiled!

Every morning I do explore
A brand new goal of life for me;
I do gather loneliness scattered
Here and there around.

Inside the folds of my pile of files
A number of thoughts are hidden
These have been noted and written
For lack of time I write on the go.

Whenever I get some time to spare
I revisit those aspects untouched
In which the elixir of life
I have mixed it in the nectar of life.

Whispering in the cupboard
Those lines come to meet me again
I wrote during my travel by train or by air
Or had kept between the bundle of papers
While rushing by car for work.

When I look for something else
in my baggage
These lines huddle together
to attract my attention.

Every morning these memories
Pay a courteous visit to me
And offer me a fitting gift
A new set of life-goals.

Along with this gift
I set out once again
With new vigour and vitality
On the path of creation
To restart my creative sojourn!

—Himalaya Bhavan, Delhi
30 May, 2021

□□□